Oh, happy birthday! You deserve a happy birthday because you make me laugh, because you love to try on new shoes, and because you know how to prune the roses. Dear friend, you deserve a perfect birthday!

Oh, happy birthday!

Oh, happy birthday!

happy birthday!

Oh, happy birthday!

...ay because you love the smell of gardenias, because you know...

...od friends, and because you remember all your...

...erve a warm...

Jenna De Angeles

14 October 2006

A Gift from the Heart

Best wishes to a remarkable woman!

To: Dr. Joan Pinkus

From: Viola (and Jonathan!)

This book is dedicated to Nicholas, Jamie, and Olivia, with special gratitude to Joseph, Mom, Dad, Melissa, and Grandma.

You Deserve a Happy Birthday!

Written and illustrated by Jenna DeAngeles

Andrews McMeel Publishing

Kansas City

You Deserve a Happy Birthday

ISBN: 0-7407-3828-3

Library of Congress Control Number: 2003100783

03 04 05 06 07 WKT 10 9 8 7 6 5 4 3 2 1

A party? A chance to celebrate you?
The kind with organza ribbons on gift boxes,
girlfriends gathered around, lilac bouquets,
a chocolate cake, and loads of fresh fruit? Perfect!
Because it's for you, the celebration will certainly
be special. Yes — YOU are the perfect reason
for a party!

Your friends have planned a party.
A festivity that lasts for an afternoon
celebrating what has taken a lifetime
to create: You!

A party because your heart is filled
with old-fashioned goodness,
because you recycle, and because
you know the names of all the flowers.
Quite simply, to celebrate your twinkle.

Every day I celebrate how you've taught me
that we can do anything — or nothing —
and still have the best time.

You've shown me how a true friendship
continues to grow season after season.
(How is it — even after spending a whole day
together — we could still talk all night long?)

Talking & Sipping

Such a good friend

Yes, a party to celebrate your free spirit.
A chance to kick up your heels
and have some fun!

The news got around of your impending
party. Of course, the sprites and fairies
wanted to drop in for the celebration.
Ladybugs and butterflies, too.
We knew you wouldn't mind, so we invited them all.

Everyone wanted to come! Maybe it is
because you appreciate staring at the stars and
running through the sprinkler. Perhaps it's because
you know what poison oak looks like when we
go on nature walks. Maybe because you know
that the number of birthdays you've had
has nothing to do with how old you are.

To celebrate the fact
you wear pink socks.

We spread the word:
A special celebration was in the wings.

To all who hold you close in their hearts,
we began to spread the word.

It took no time at all to prepare a
guest list: You are so loved!

We gathered your friends who love to laugh so hard their stomachs hurt, who cherish your cozy home, who appreciate your cookbook collection.
We invited your friends who like sitting on the porch eating chocolate-covered strawberries.

This was going to be something special.

Celebrate! Come celebrate for a day.
Keep the memories for life.

Because you always have an aspirin in
your purse, because you save aluminum foil if
it's still clean, because you think anything
homemade is better than store-bought,
because you are an authentic friend,
we wanted to have this little gathering.

We spread the word around the world.

From exotic lands far and away . . .

to places of simple beauty . . .

to tropical lands of
hibiscus and pineapples . . .

to lands of mystery, we sent invitations.

Everyone said, "Of course we'll come!
Wouldn't miss it for the world!"

We traveled around the globe and then . . .
it was a good time for a nap.

Dream
Sweet
Dreams

"Leap out of bed!" we giggled with joy!
"Look your best! The countdown begins now!"
In just a matter of minutes we gave
ourselves days of duties. What fun!
Everything from ribbons to blooms,
petit fours to perfume,
something grand was growing.

We knew in an instant what would
warm your heart:
Charming prints. Polka dots.
Curling ribbon and satin bows.
We tied, beaded, trimmed, and tucked.

And we snickered a lot.

Music for mood, lighting for effect.
We wanted it all to be perfect.
We wanted you to enjoy every detail,
to notice every moment.

We had special help
decorating your cake. Not too sweet,
not too frilly or too gussied up.
"Just enough" was our motto
(but it had to be chocolate).

We draped garlands,
we tied them with taffeta.
We learned, no matter what the occasion,
you can never have too many flowers . . .
or too many friends.

Because you buy wildflower seeds
and toss them out the car,
because you like to scrub your oven,
because you actually made
peanut butter once . . .these are the reasons why
you deserve a happy birthday.

Because you never show up empty-handed,
because you bake blackberry cobblers,
because you have your priorities straight . . .

because you love your country, and you know
how to make Shirley Temples for the kids,
because weeping willows are your favorite tree . . .

and
that I
love

because your smile lights up the room,
because, makeup or not,
you are always beautiful.

The fairies volunteered to light the way.
No detail was forgotten.
No expense spared.

Yep, we splurged,
we indulged,
we were enlightened!

When we finished planning it all,
we took some time to reflect.
It was heaven.

Now, yes now, we were ready
to throw a splendid party!

Such joy filled the air: Gardenias and angels,
giggles and streamers . . . it was a real party.

A celebration fit for a queen.
And for you, only the most royal treatment.

A time to celebrate!
To pretend you're a balloon
and pop with pleasure!

Happy Day!!

Have a fairy happy birthday!

Many blessings

Do silly things, laugh until
your cheeks hurt, pretend you're
a kid again, and wear paper hats!
Celebrate!

Happy Birthday!

We celebrate you because you love
heart-shaped cookie cutters,
wreaths on your front door,
the ice-cream man,
pink blossoms, and opening presents.

Because you twinkle.

We happen to be the luckiest ones
on your birthday . . .
because you are truly the greatest gift.

We celebrate you since the day you were born, from the moment you took your first breath. When the angels blessed your arrival, on your very first birthday, it was decided . . .

you deserve a happy birthday each and every year.